James Joel Cartwright

Papers Relating to the Delinquency of Lord Savile, 1642-1646

James Joel Cartwright

Papers Relating to the Delinquency of Lord Savile, 1642-1646

ISBN/EAN: 9783337312220

Printed in Europe, USA, Canada, Australia, Japan

Cover: Foto ©ninafisch / pixelio.de

More available books at **www.hansebooks.com**

THE CAMDEN MISCELLANY,

VOLUME THE EIGHTH:

CONTAINING

FOUR LETTERS OF LORD WENTWORTH, AFTERWARDS EARL OF STRAFFORD, WITH A POEM ON HIS ILLNESS.

MEMOIR BY MADAME DE MOTTEVILLE ON THE LIFE OF HENRIETTA MARIA.

PAPERS RELATING TO THE DELINQUENCY OF LORD SAVILE, 1642-1646.

A SECRET NEGOCIATION WITH CHARLES THE FIRST, 1643-1644.

A LETTER FROM THE EARL OF MANCHESTER ON THE CONDUCT OF CROMWELL.

LETTERS ADDRESSED TO THE EARL OF LAUDERDALE.

ORIGINAL LETTERS OF THE DUKE OF MONMOUTH.

CORRESPONDENCE OF THE FAMILY OF HADDOCK 1657-1719.

LETTERS OF RICHARD THOMPSON TO HENRY THOMPSON, OF ESCRICK, CO. YORK.

PRINTED FOR THE CAMDEN SOCIETY.

M.DCCC.LXXXIII.

PAPERS RELATING

TO THE

DELINQUENCY OF LORD SAVILE.

1642–1646.

EDITED BY

JAMES J. CARTWRIGHT, M.A., F.S.A.,

TREASURER OF THE SOCIETY.

PRINTED FOR THE CAMDEN SOCIETY.

M.DCCC.LXXXIII.

INTRODUCTION.

Thomas, Viscount Savile, was the son of Sir John Savile, of Howley, Member for Yorkshire, who was one of the earliest opponents of Wentworth, afterwards Earl of Strafford, both in that county and in Parliament. Sir John was created Baron Savile, of Pontefract, on the same day, viz. 21 July, 1628, that Wentworth obtained his first step in the peerage; his death occurred on 31 August, 1630. His son and heir, Thomas, became attached to the court of Charles, first as Controller and afterwards as Treasurer of the Household. Lord Clarendon described him as a man of an ambitious and restless nature; of parts and wit enough; but, in his disposition and inclination, so false, that he could never be believed or depended upon. Thomas Savile inherited his father's hatred of Wentworth and lost no chance of doing him a mischief. With this object he is said to have been the chief means of inducing the Scots to march an army into England in 1640; and the grave charge was brought against him of having forged a letter from some of the English nobility to the Scots Commissioners inviting them to enter the kingdom. His private confession of this plot to Charles gained him much favour; but on the King's coming to York, writes Clarendon, the county in which Savile's fortune and interest lay, his reputation was so low that none of the gentlemen of position there would hold any communication with him. His subsequent proceedings are best gathered from the papers here printed, the originals of which are preserved in the Public Record Office, London, and the Bodleian Library, Oxford. In May, 1644, the King created him Earl of Sussex, but the Parliament does not appear to have recognised the title, which ultimately descended to his son James and became extinct in 1671. The family estates went through female descendants into the hands of the Earls of Cardigan. Lord Savile's seat at Howley, near Morley, in Yorkshire, so frequently referred to in these papers, is now a ruin, having been demolished in 1731 by Lord Cardigan to save, it is said, the great cost of maintaining it. Burke, in his Extinct Peerage, puts down Lord Savile's death as having occurred in 1646; and this date has been accepted without question by later writers. It is, however, clearly a mistake. In a paper here printed, dated in August, 1646, he speaks of himself as childless, his second marriage having taken place about 1641; at the time of his death there is no doubt he had both a son and daughter living. Local evidence also exists that in 1650 he granted a lease of the Old Chapel in Morley to the Presbyterians. The Journals of the House of Commons contain references to him as a living person of a much later date than 1646; and among the Royalist Composition Papers is a petition from him not thought necessary to give in this collection, which is undated, but is distinctly referred to in another document as having been presented by Lord Savile on 31 January, 1652-3. Scatcherd, the historian of Morley, sets down his death as having probably occurred in 1661, but no positive evidence of the date has hitherto been brought to light.

The statement at page 2 is valuable as giving direct evidence of the authorship of the Petition of the Peers, which has hitherto been believed to have been the work of Pym alone, but which is here shown to have been drawn up by Pym and St. John.

J. J. C.

PAPERS RELATING

DELINQUENCY OF LORD SAVILE.

Lord Savile to Lady Temple.[a]

[Royalist Composition Papers, Second Series, vol. vi.]

My Ladie Temple,   [November, 1642.]

I was verie much troubled at a report I had y^t yor house was visited wth ye plague, but am exceeding glad to heare so well of it now, as my Cosen Bland[b] assures me, by a letter from yo^{r}selfe, in wch letter shee saith you write y^t you are sorie to heare y^t I have absolutelie declared my self ag^t the pliam^t, wch I wonder at this time to heare, when all the gentlemen of this countie complaine of me to the King for being to affectionate to the pliam^t. And I am confident y^t Sr John Hotham himselfe will say otherwaies of me then you are enformed.

But it hath beene my fortune still, ever to receive worst usage where I thought y^t I had best deserved, and never more aparent then in the dealing w^{ch} (by misenformation I hope) the parliament hath done to me. To you I may wthout vaunting say, that if this

---

[a] Sir Peter Temple, of Stowe, married for his second wife, Christian, daughter of Sir John Leveson, of Trentham. Whitelocke, in his *Memorials*, describes this Lady Temple as a busy woman, and a great politician, who had acted as the agent and messenger of Lord Savile.

[b] The writer's sister, Katherine, married Sir Thomas Bland, of Kippax Park.

CAMD. SOC.   B

parliam^t have done anie greate matters for ye publique, ore are in a condition more free then other parliam^{ts}, God wch governes all things, and knowes all secretts, knowes this, that if I were not at first the . onelie, yet I was (though unworthie) his chiefest, instrum^t to bring it to pass. I never so much as differd from them in anie thing whilst there was a syllable of the petition ungranted wch wee delivered at Yorke, and was drawne, as you know, by Mr. Pymm himselfe and Mr. Sollicitor. And so farr onelie wee were obliged by covenant amongst oureselfes. For there alterations wch they now desire in the Church, let my Lo. Say and Brooke witnes for me, if ever I was for it in my life; and therefore in a free pliam^t why it was not lawfull for me to vote freelie, according to my conscience, wthout to be made of ye malignant partie, I could not imagine. Was there ever anie good message wch they ever had from ye King but something I contributed to it? Was there ever anie violent one but I oposed it? The message at Windsor, where ye K. granted the militia, I drew (which I have often hard of). When my Lo. Howard and Sir Philipp Stapleton was at Yorke, let them report of me what my part was; what I did wth the King at Bev^{r}ley, when myLord of Holland and Sir Ph. Stapleton brought the overture of peace, let them and all the courte report. The message at Nottingham, where the King offered to take downe his standard, dismiss his forces, and recall his pclamations, all the lordes know y^t I both persuaded it, and wth my owne handes, by the King's pmission, drew it up. My Lord of Cumberlande's Comission I protested against, made my name be putt out of it, and where there was a clause to enable him to levie money uppon the countie, in the open assemblie of the gentlemen I declamed against it as being ag^t the law and subiectes libertie, for w^{ch}, as my Lord of Dorsit and others know, I was complained of to the King. Now I would faine know for wch of these actes I am forbidden to sitt in parliam^t and declared an enemie to the publique. Was I found guiltie of bringing up the armie ag^t the parliam^t, or privie to the Kings going into the Howse of Commons? Was I so much as privie much less psuading to his leaving y⁸ parliamᵗ, and going to Yorke? Was I not against both his going agᵗ Hull, Coventrie, and Warwick? Have I taken anie commaund in the armie in this unnaturall warr? Did I not retire to my owne howse (when the King broke up his house, so as my attendance and oath tied me no longer) in peace and quiett, and when I could do no further good, yet would not contribute to anie of the fatall evills wᶜʰ must follow? Do I not at this time heere protect all ministers and others yᵗ pfess religion from yᵉ violence of the times, so farr as to render me suspected to all my frendes? Now, my Ladie Temple, iudge yᵗ when men yᵗ have done the contrarie to all yᵉ good yᵗ I have done, have done as much agᵗ the meeting of this pliaᵗ as I have done for it, as much agᵗ peace as I have done for it, have taken armes, commandes, agᵗ the parliamᵗ, and still continew so; have given publique and violent counsells when I gave peaceable ones ; yet not a man but myself, that I know this day in England (without any impeachmᵗ or calling to answer), is forbidden the pliament howse, and stigmatized wᵗʰ the name of enemie to the publique. I never yet could learne yᵗ ever they had anie thing agᵗ me to balance all the good offices wᶜʰ I have done, but these 2 thinges onelie: the comminge downe to Yorke wᵗʰout leave, and contrarie to there order, and for what I did at Heworth Moore, in Yorkeshire, when the countie was assembled there by the King's commaund; to both wᶜʰ thus much. The oath which I tooke as Tresorer of yᵉ King's howse is flatt and plaine, to serve his Maᵗⁱᵉ in yᵗ office in his howse and not to departe wᵗʰout his espetiall licence had and obteigned first. As long as I could by anie mediation prvaile wᵗʰ the King to let me stay at yᵉ parliamᵗ I did stay when he pemptorilie under his owne hand, both uppon paine of my allegiance, and my oathe taken, charged me to come downe and do my sʳvice in his howse. I durst not forsweare my selfe, but came accordinglie and staied wᵗʰ him whilst his household continued, and then went home; for I was shutt out of the pliamᵗ by a vote before, my offence being that I durst not forsweare my selfe positivelie to obey an order, though manie went contrarie to there order (no oath compelling them neither), wch for all that have no such sentence. For y^t of Heworth Moore, wch they declared me an enemie to the publique for doing, thus in breife:—Before my coming to Yorke the King had apoynted y^t meeting; and y^t morning I, finding that the devided people entended to have pressed 2 petitions contrarie one to another uppon the King, wch in such a mightie concourse of people might have ended in violence, and knowing that those who they terme the good partie, and who came fearefullie under my assurance and ptection, were farr ye lesser number, I called to me John Reyner, Mr. Farer, Mr. Todd, Mr. Rigeley, and all the heades of that partie, and told them y^t if they would assure me that there side would deliver no petition, I would take such order that the other should not. They repaired to there partie, and assured me there should be none delivered by them; and so wee went to the field, and finding Sr John Bourchier reading, as they said, a petition (though it was none), I, conceving he did it in ignorance of oure agreem^t, and contrarie to the will of the honest men of his side, tooke it from him. And now behold ye act y^t makes me an enemie of ye Commonwealth. I have beene long in these expressions, because I desire you would let them be knowne, though not openlie publish my letter. To the truth of all in it God is witnes, and men allso. Madam, I am

Yo^r faithfull freind,
SAVILE.

Commend my service to my Ladie Carli[sle and ?] Bedford, and all my frendes, and particularlie to my poore Cozen Carr and his wife, whose busines I am afraide may miscarie by reason of my absence from the courte, which greives me much.

———————

THE SAME TO THE SAME.

MA.

I shall ever augnowledge you have done me the office of a frend, and in that way wherin I most valew frendshipp, that is in good offices to the parliam^t, towards whome, though I know my owne harte, how it is and ever hath beene sett, yet it is now a greate office of frendshipp to make one to be understood as he is. Comend my service to my Lord Sey and to noble Sir Ph. Stapleton, and assure them that I will never forgett ye publique nor these pticuler favoures (if it please God to leave me anie power). Tell my Lo. Scy y^t peradventure he may be as falselie represented where I am at the courte, as I may be where he is at the parliam^t. I desire but the same iustice from him there as he shall be sure to find from me heere, and to believe thus of me, that either I will see such an acomodation as I may live in court in the fellowshipp of noble, vertuous, and deserving persons, or at least not at all wth such persons (whome he may imagine) y^t shall beare sway. For anie honor to be done to the howse by anie augnowledgm^t of mine I shall never grudge, nor thinke I took anie honor y^t the howse gaines by me. My hart should second my wishes in comming to you, but y^t this bearer can tell you how strictlie wee are beseiged heere, so as not so much as a serving man, much less my selfe, can yet stirr one mile out of towne. And wch is most miserable, oure deliverance in probabilitie must come by my Lord of Newcastle's forces, manie of which are Papists as his declaration (wch I presume you have seene) will let you understand : all which doth leade me into the consideration of those unspeakable miseries which this once flourishing contrie doth now grone under. First Sr John Hotham's and ye Lincolnshire forces called to his assistance under the pretence of setling the militia and seazing of delinquents, this countie (I will speake faithfullie) hath been robbed of and impoverished above a hundred thowsand pound wthin this little space, and . . . . . manie licentious plunderings and villanies committed as are incredible, and wch I am loth to name, because done under the sacred name of parliament; and to say truth according to there power, much after the same manner done by oures. And to remedie all this and to make the mesure of there suffrings full the loosing side is glad to call in my Lord of Newcastle wth 6,000 men qualified as aforesaid ; and padventure my Lord of Derbie allso, if t'other be not sufficient, will be called in allso, to do as much for the one part as hath allreadie been don to the other, and so leave no one pson between them that shall not be made miserable, ruined, and undone, besides an occasion given the Romanistes to assemble in a bodie together. For preventing of this miserie I am now as active as I can; and if I can prevaile and y^t anie reason will satisfie the parliam^t forces, wee will endure it rather than admitt this cure, wch being effected or attempted to my power, if I can gett by anie meanes away, you shall see me shortlie after; and in the meane space I will be preparing and shall ever rest

Your faithfull frend and servant.

The Same to the Same.

MADAM,   [December, 1642.]

I did receive youre letter, which was dated the 29 of Octob. uppon the 10 of November, so it had a verie slow passage. All letters are now opened, so I am glad to disguise my hand neither with superscription nor subscription; the bearer will know who to deliver it unto, and you will then easilie guess from whome it comes. You desire to know what my aimes and intentions are, that my frendes may do me service. I answer, the same they ever was; since you let in my Lord Lowden, I would not have the K. trample on ye pliam^t nor the pliament lessen him so much as to make a way for the people to rule us all. I hate papists so much as I would not have the King necessetated to use them for his defence, nor owe anie obligation unto them. I love religion so well as I would not have it putt to the hazard of a battle. I love libertie so much that I would not trust it in the handes of a conqueror. For as much as I love the King, I should not be glad he beate the pliam^t, though they were in the wrong. I would do all good offices I could for the parliam^t, and me thinkes I could do manie wthout loosing either my conscience or my master. If they would give me leave and if I might uppon those faire and Christian termes, I would be glad to come to my house at London, where I should be able to enlarge myselfe further then now I dare where nothing can pass wthout search. Madam, you see, as I ever did, that I speake freelie, and not as biased nor enclined by the pliam^{ts} success; for wee heere are assured the K. is prosperous at this time neere London. The Q.* wee heare, last night landed at Newcastle with great supplies from Denmarke. My Lo. of Newcastle and wee heere have almost ten thousand men together; and yet my desires are still the same to have no conquests of either side, nor shall ever desire to live to see the ruine of an English parliam^t. I will say it once againe, if I may safelie and honorablie come to London, I doupt not but they shall find there worst frend is not com.

Since I writt first unto you Mr. Hotham (when I litle expected such a comand) by a command from ye parliam^t, as he saith, hath seased on my howse, and all I have, to the valew of som 1,300l. in money and goodes, and yet threatens to deface the carcase of Howley. Whether I have deserved this usage God will determine one day, and how iust it is the aughters will feele.

I am infinitelie glad, for all this that my Cleopatra is recovered, that all youres are well, and would be mightie glad to see both my cozen Carrs.

[Cover addressed: "For La. Te. Lincolne Ins feildes."]

---

* The Queen landed from Holland at Bridlington at the end of Feb. 1643.

THE KING TO THE EARL OF NEWCASTLE.

[Draft in the handwriting of Sir Edward Nicholas. Clarendon MSS. 1682.]

RT. TRUSTY,

Having receav[ed] and perused the charge against our right trusty, the Lo[rd] V[iscount] Savile, and being resolved ourselfe in person to hear him answer to the same : our w[ill] and command is that you forthwith give order to the Governor of Newark for his present release, and because the wayes are full of souldiers we will that you cause the said governor to allow such a convoye to conduct him hither as he shall desire to prevent him being intercepted by any forces of the rebells, for which.

Given Oxon.

13° Maii, 1643.

E. Newcastle.

INFORMATIONS AGAINST THE LORD VISCOUNT SAVILE.

[Clarendon MSS. 1688.]

First it is affirmed by gentlemen of quality and will bee proued that hee before my cominge into the country, and when the enemy had confined them to the city of Yorke, his publique vote and opinion was, that it was best for them and for the peace of their countrey to deliuer upp the citty of Yorke into the Rebells hands, or words to that effect, which I neuer heard of till long after I had conferred the place of Gouernour upon him, which begatt such a generall jealousy in most of the gentry, and besides such a generall feare amongst them at Yorke, that it shold be deliuered upp, that I cold not thincke it safe to continew him in that place.

Secondly there was brought mee part of a letter from my Lord Sauile directed to Mr. John Hotham or Sir John Hotham, in these words :—

I neyther left furniture of use, nor any prouision without doores, besides all my beare in my seller, are by the guards and others druncke of, soe as for the present I am compelled to bee here at the mannour of Yorke, and shall presume of your noble curtesy for the convoy of my wife hether, and protection from feare when shee is here as you were pleased to offer mee before. And I doe desire also you wilbee pleased giue mee a passe to goe to Skipton to her, or my owne howse at Howley, to provide it ready assoone as I can, for if you keepe Yorke soe close about as you doe wee shall haue but short commons here shortly. Sir, 1 hope you wilbee pleased so[a] worke about, as that it may bee in your power onely to dispose of mee, wherein you shall finde mee, both now and hereafter,

Your faithful friend and seruant,

SAUILE.

Thirdly, I send a letter dated the 24th of December from Grayes Inne from Wm. Risley to the Lord Viscount Sauile exprest in mistical tearmes which I leave to interpretation.

Fourthly, there was a letter writt from a gent. of quallity beinge at Leedes to Sir Marmaduke Langdale, being then att Pontifract, which amongst other things had this exposition: about a weeke agoe I receaued from his Excellence a command to send 30^{ty} muskitiers to Howley to my Lord Sauile's howse to bee com- *These musket-manded by some of his servants, which I did acordingly, and this ires here re-turned back day at dinner they came hether and said Sir Thomas Fairfax hath to give the sent word that the howse and parke shold bee safe, and soe my enemy's forces place. Lord Sauile had given order to send them to their quarters, I pray you acquaint his Excellence therewith.

Fifthly, I have received a letter from a gent. of quality from Leedes, which amongst other things is conteined as followeth: My Lord, I have received your Excellence his letter, and doe

* *Sic.*

conceive you doe expect from mee what I know concerning my
Lord Sauile's howse, by any command from the enemie; the trueth
is, it came not to mee as a secrett. If your Excellence send to Mr.
Copley at Doncaster, my Lord Sauile's nephew, or M^r. Bonnicar at
Howley, they can tell you that my Lord Sauile is assured from the
enemy that neyther his howse nor partie shalbee troubled. And I
heare that the enemy hath sent to see whether it was not fitt for them
to putt some men into the howse, it lyinge upon a convenient
passage from Bradford, etc.

Sixthly, I saw a letter from a gent of quality to the Maior-
Generall Sir Francis Mackworth, as followeth: In this night,
betwixt sonne sett and day breake, Bradforde men sent sixty musketiers, and put them into my Lord Sauile's house at Howley; they
was brought thether by the Lord Sauile's steward, and it is thought
with my Lord Sauile's consent. This howse is foure myles distant
from this towne (meaninge Wakefeild), and in the way to Bradford.
Three troopes of horse came with them. I sent to Howley to
bee certainely informed, and they brought mee answer that it was
thought the troopes were retourned backe.

Seauenthly, I received and have a letter from a gent of quality of
the 17th of January, 1642, directed to myselfe, as followes, amongst
other things: This morneinge one Elizabeth Cade, of Woodchurch,
giveth this information to mee, that the last night about twylight
some 250 foote and horse came to Howley, my Lord Sauile's howse,
and so soone as they came, William Birkby and Michaell Midle-
borrow, my lord's cheife servants, did with all the kindness possible
enterteine them, and the principall men that came with them where
three of the Greatheades. And they that went to fetch them were
Richard Burnely, William Sparlinge, and Richard Scott, all being
my Lord Sauile's tennants, and Nicholas Greathead said to one
Rose, an old servant to the howse, that my lord was now tourned
to their side.

Eighthly, I saw a letter to Sir Edward Osborne and Sir Marmaduke Langdale from a gent of quality, as follows: That hee was

informed the Lord Sauile's howse was taken, and 60ᵗʸ musketiers of the enemies put into itt; whereupon hee sent three gent thether to bring him certaine knowledge thereof, and they retourned it so, and that the Lord Sauile's steward did come thether with them, and it is thought with the Lord Sauile's consent.

Ninthly, it is confessed, if not will bee proued, that my Lord Sauile gave Mr. Hotham 200ˡⁱ.

And if it bee objected that displaceing of him had beene sufficient to satisfy the peoples jealousy, I answere as these tymes are, wee had not need to give those that are likely to bee against his Majestie's seruice liberty to excercise their power, which would bee made worse by being displeased.

Answer to the Informations against the Lord Viscount Savile.

[Clarendon MSS. 1690.]

To the first, where it is sayd to be affirmed, and wilbe proued, that before the Earle of Newcastle's comming into Yorkshire he did publiquely vote to deliuer the citty of Yorke into the Rebell's hands: Its answerd that there was neuer any such thing put to the vote to his remembrance, neither did he ever deliuer any such opinion: but doth appeale to my Lᵈ of Cumberland, and the gentlemen of that countie, for his justification herein, and 'tis to be presumed that my Lᵈ of Cumberland is a man of such honor and trust that he would not have heard any such opinion from a person of the Lᵈ Sauil's qualitie without acquainting his Maᵗʸ with it, at least, if he did noe more, and he is verie sure that whosomeuer was earnest for my Lᵈ Newcastle's comming in, could not be of that opinion.

For the E. of Newcastle's conferring the gouvernment of Yorke uppon the Lᵈ Sauile, it was doen iust at his Lorᵖᵖˢ parting from Yorke to Tadcaster, and not known to the Ld Sauile untill the instant of his goeing; and when my Ld Sauile heard from his L^pp of this letter and other iealousies he did humbly desir, at Pomfret, that this gouvernment might be disposed of into some other hand, protesting that he should take it no way unkindlie: but my L^d of Newcastle seemed then soe well satisfied concerning the letter, and all other things, that he was pleased to say that he would offer my Ld Sauile soe much violence (as he term'd it) to continue him ther, whether he would or noe; and so he did retourne him to that charge with greater trust then he had before, and doth a little wonder that what then was not thought worthy any reproofe, should since cause his imprizonment: but my Ld Sauile complaines not of it, since this hath given him the opportunitie to cleere himselfe to his Ma^ty.

To the second, he confesses he did write a letter to Hotham: but it was with the privitie of my Lord of Cumberland for a conuoye for his lady and her servants, who was then at his Lordshipps house at Skipton, wherein he might say, to devert the ennymie from rifling his house, which was in ther power, that ther was at that tyme in it neither furniture of vallewe, nor provisions of beare, or victualls, which might inuite soldiers thether. And for the clawse in the letter, that they should have short commons in Yorke shortlie, he appeals to the gent. in Yorke, whether it was not ther designe to make the ennymie belieue they were in danger of famine, which they feared not, to avoyd an assault, which they feared; and then were directed on purpose, as can be proued, to brute the necessities of victuall, which is notoriously knowne they abounded in, to the end the ennymie might set quiet in that expectation, untill they were relieued, which was then assured to be souddainly, etc.; besides the Ld Sauile did acquaint some gent. publiquely at an ordinarie with that particular clawse of his letter and the reasons of it. For that other clawse, when the Ld Sauile desires Hotham soe to worke about, as that it might bee in his power only to dispose of him, it was uppon this occasion Hotham denyed the Ld Sauils sister, the

Lady Bland, to give any quarter to his house, because he was a man proscribed by the parliam[t], and only excepted in his commission which he had from the parlm[t]. But told her, if my Lord would take the courtesie from him and not be beholding to my L[d] Fairfax, nor any other for it, he would send to the parlm[t] for power to spare the house, all which wilbe made appeere by Hotham's owne letters, that there agreement was only for the saueguard of the house at Howley, and nothing else besides.

To the third, concerning Rislye's letter, he was a man sent to Mr. Sec[rie] Nicholas to Oxford about my L[d] Sauil's goeing to London with instructions, that if he could by his reasons make it appeere to Mr. Sec[rie] that the L[d] Sauil's goeing thether could be for his Ma[ties] seruice, and he might haue his Ma[ties] approbation, then he would goe, and not otherwise, and the token that the L[d] Sauile was to know it by was this, either affirmative in putting in a chancerie bill, if 'twere consented to, or negatiuely if 'twere denyed; and of the truth of this appeale is made to Sec[rie] Nicholas he write[a] negatiuely. Soe the L[d] Sauile understood his Ma[ties] mind and went not. Diuers of these letters the L[d] Sauile receau'd, for he wrot manie least some might miscarry.

To the fowrth 'tis answerd that the L[d] Sauile haueing 10,000[li] worth of plate, iewles, and goods in his house at Howley, he desired of the E. of Newcastle a guard of 30 musquetiers to secure the house, which was granted; but after that by a conuoye of horsse sent by Generall Goring, all the vallewable goods were brought to Yorke. Captaine Copley came to my L[d] Sauile and informed him that Sir W[m] Sauile (then gouernour of Leeds) wanted these men, and that the neighbors therabouts (who v ere molested by these soldiers) would rather take uppon them the defence of the house and parke then suffer soe much as they did by these soldiers; wher uppon my L[d] Sauile wrot to Sir W[m] Sauile that he might remoue them if he pleased. What the musquetiers sayd at ther retourn the L[d] Sauile knows not, neither it is[a] much materiall that being no

[a] *Sic.*

profe ; but sure it is the Ld Sauile know not of any such engage-
ment of Sir Thom. Fairfax as is spoken of, and the euent shewes
the contrary; for since they have both taken and defaced the house,
consumed corne, hay, and all the stock, destroy'd both parkes about
it, receaued his rent and reuenues, and this without any late offence
of my Ld Sauile, who hath bine euer since a prisoner; soe as either
Sir Thom. Fairfax kept his word ill (if he made any such promise)
or the Ld Sauile, who was then a prisoner in Newarke Castle (and
knew not that his house was taken untill long after), had a verie ill
bargaine of itt, who euer made it.

To the 5th, 6th, 7th, and 8th, all which are onlie relations of certaine letters of unknown persons concerneing the takeing of the
house at Howley and ther opinions, that it was done with the
Sauil's^a consent, 'tis answerd as before, being done after he was
prizoner, and that he was so far from being consenting to it as that
he did not soe much as know it untill long after it was done, and
then receaued it as the saddest news he ever had in his life, loosing
by it the bewtie of his house, parkes, and possession of his goods
and reuenewes, which was to mentaine him and his. With what
kindnesse any of the Ld Sauil's tennants entertained the ennymies,
either for loue or feare, is nothing material at all to him, it being
well known to all Yorkshire that many of his tennants and of other
men's are fauorers of that cause, and doe pay euen his rents to the
ennymies, which surely none will belieue to be done with his
consent; but, to say the truth, ther are few in the West Riding
(my L^d of Cumberland's tennants not excepted) who doe not in this
case play the knaues. What he was that told old Rose that my
Ld Sauile was turned to ther side matters not much, since 'tis likely
when he was a prisoner many might iudge it was for fauoring
ther party; but the Ld Sauile doth challenge any profe whatsomever that either in letters, treatie, or any other way, he did euer soe
much as intimate a thought to desert the King's cause, for support-
ing which he hath lost all the estate he had.

^a Sic.

For the 9th 'tis answerd after he had defended his house from
Lowinger's assault, wounded him and diuers with him, he was
commanded by the E. of Cumberland to assist him at Yorke, and
his house was left in the custody of his sister, the Lady Bland, with
these instructions, that the men in it should defend it untill cannon
were brought against it, and then according to his Maties permission
(given at Nottingham to the Ld Savile, Sir Edward Osborne, and
Sir Francis Muncton) to compound the best she could. Our men
being forced out of Leedes, they marched with their army towards
Howley, a house that cost 30,000^{li} the building, and hauing at that
tyme in it to the vallewe of 10,000^{li} in goods, plate, &c. The Lady
Bland with much a doe obtained of Mr. Hotham (by promising a
some of mony to the soldiers that were hurt before it) respit that
it should not be plundred at that tyme; though, as Hotham said, it
was beyond his commission so to do, yet he promised to send up to
the parliam^t for power to doe it. This mony, 'tis belieued, the
Lady Bland did pay uppon this extremity, and the Ld Sauile will
not denye, but he was glad of it, when he knew it, to haue his
house and goods saued soe, rather then to be ruined by the ennymie;
and this was a thing generally know", or familiarlie debated at
Pomfret, long before my Ld Sauil's restraint, betweene the E. of
Newcastle and him, and in the presence of many gentlemen of the
countrie, and neuer obiected as a fault untill now.

Lastlie, if the displacing of the Ld Sauile would haue quenched
jealousies, the E. of Newcastle knowes how earnestly his Lo^{pp} was
desired by the Ld Sauile at Pomfret to doe it for that cause, that
gouvernement in his hands, if it were not for his Maties seruice
being but soe much unnecessarie care and trouble to himselfe ; but
it seemes it was thought better in this manner to remoue him
then at his own request. But my Ld Sauile is farr from belieueing
this to be the act of the E. of Newcastle, and doth assure himselfe
it proceeded from the wrongful information of some other personnes,
he having receiued such assurances of the E. of Newcastle's good
affection as that he can not in honor doubt of them.

Sir Edward Nicholas to the Earl of Newcastle.

[Clarendon MSS. 1695.]

As wee found in the charge against the Ld Sauile very good cause of suspicion *and ground for what you did*, so have wee receaved from him soe full and cleere an aunsweare as wee have not whereto to reply; but yet wee thought not fitt to accept his aunsweare as satisfactory till wee had sent the same to you and receaved from you your opinion of it, or what may be further said to it, which when wee shall understand from you wee shall then soone make our determinate iudgment upon it ; and therefore wee desire to heere from yow in this particular with as much diligence as conveniently you may.

Given att Oxen 5° Junii, 1643.

E. Newcastle.

Reply of the Earl of Sussex to the Charges brought against him by the King.

[Clarendon MSS. 1820.]

[January, 1645.]

It is most true that in my peticion I doe urge the breach of the liberties of parliament, notwithstanding his Maties promise engaged to the contrary. But I add that I assuredly beleeue it was unknowne to his Ma^ty, by which I meant that his Matie conceived, that without acquainting the House of Peeres before, and desyring that upon such reasons such persons might be secured, hee might by his owne speciall command have done it without breach of priviledges of parliament. I did humbly conceive otherwaies, and that although his Ma^ty did not knowe soe much, yett it was against the essentiall priviledges of the House.

1. That I am very sory that his Ma^{ty} hath been so misinformed as that I should att any tymes deny the proteccion or vilify the power and jurisdiccion of the Lords heere assembled, which I both doe and shall euer honour and study to preserue. But, peraduenture, I may have sayd (though I doe not remember) somthing concerning their jurisdiccion as the House of Peeres untill themselves should please to declare themselues so, but never doubted they had now as much priviledge as if they were so, in regard his Ma^{ty} hath been so gracious as to have granted it unto them.

2. 'Tis true that whilst I was in the North the Marques of Newcastle, hauing by some malicious persons beene informed that I had a designe to sease on the Queenes Maties person when shee should land, did sease on my person at night and hurried me to Newarke Castle, where I remained close prisoner 26 weekes. How many tymes I pressed his Ma^{ty} to haue a tryall, by many letters to my Lord of Falkland, I knowe his Ma^{ty} well remembers. How assuredly he was made belieue that I had such a designe against the Queenes Ma^{ty} doth well appeare by his Ma^{ts} owne writing to the Queene (which shee hath since told me) how great a danger shee escaped in not comming when shee intended to doe. At last my tryall was granted, and I sent for to Oxford to answer the Marques of Newcastle's charge, in which was not one syllable of that great crime I was committed for, but some (as I may modestly say) other fragments collected to make a charge against mee, which I answered in halfe an howers space to the full satisfaccion of his Matie, as in his letter to my Lord Newcastle hee expressed, unto whome my answere was sent to see if hee could reply unto it ; who returned his Ma^{ty} a letter that he had nothing to reply against that answere, but should be heartily glad of any grace or favour his Ma^{ty} should doe my Lord Sauile ; and hath most nobly and ingenuously since in a great assembly asked mee pardon for that commitment, saying he was ashamed to looke mee in the face, that he would with his life and fortune giue mee any satisfaccion he could, and named unto mee the particular persons that was the cause of doing me that

violence and the suggesters of that groundles crime. And I am confident I am, in the opinion of that noble Lord, at this instant as cleere from any suspition of disloyalty or disaffiction as any person living, and therefore doe wonder that this which hath been soe fully allready answered, and, if there were any error committed, is since, by his Maties sealed pardon as well as his verball, remitted, should nowe be questioned. But I doe not mencion the sayd pardon as to thinke that action deserved any, but am ready againe either to produce my old answere or to make another as his Matie shall thinke fitt. I knowe very assuredly noe dishonour can touch me in that busines, which is so well knowne to many. And for the wordes that Sir John Hotham should say, I doe beleeve to be sayd because his Matie avowes it ; but that any man that knowes how infamous, how inconstant, how detestable a traytor that man was, I hope his words will bee of no value or esteeme. When he returned to his allegeance I knowe not, but I have assuredly heard that at his death hee tooke it, that all the pretences hee made to the King was but further to serve the parliament by him.

3. I doe say, upon my honor, that since my comming to Oxford, I doe not knowe whether Sir Peter Temple or my Lady bee living, and that excepting to my wife and for money, cloathes, and accommodacions for her, I haue neither written letter, nor received any, sent message nor received any from them nor any person living of the enimies party, which I beleeue fewe in this Towne can say besydes my selfe. But it was my resolucion to keepe my selfe soe cleere, as doubting how many evill eyes I had upon mee. But if this correspondence be meant by my Lady Temple when I was at York, with which I did acquaint his Ma^{ty} and Secretary Nicholas, withall, and which was lykewise charged by my Lord of Newcastle, but upon his Ma^{ts} owne knowledge of the thinge, and Mr. Secretary Nicholas discharged, if yett his Ma^{ty} shall require a newe answere unto it, he shall be glad of the occasion, as well knowing that as often as that busines shall bee layd open, so often shall my integritie, sinceritie, and loyalty be manifested. And concerning

what he hath done by his agents he doth lykewise protest upon his honour, that he never gave direction to any person living, to give any such intelligence as in the charge is mencioned, neither did nor doth know of any that ever did.

4. Hee understands this to be that old peece of letter written to Captaine Hotham, mencioned before in my Lord of Newcastle's charge, and therefore does refer it to that answere. But how I may have been represented to the Close Committee, to bee theyr friend, and for what reasons I stay heere, I doe not know. But I am sure I gave no cause for it, for I protest before God I doe not so much as know who they are which bee of that committee; never received, never sent the least message, letter, or had any intelligence whatsomever with them; and upon this issue will he venture his life.

5. If the persons were named that I should goe about to corrupt in theyr affections to his Ma^{ty}, or the speeches which I should say were used by his Ma^{ty} against them, I should giue a more particular answere to this charge. Now only in the generall I must say this, that I have euer endeavoured to increase his Maties partye (as God knowes), never to diminish it; that it was neuer in my heart to doe so false and meane a thing as this, nor euer in my toung. I am ashamed to utter it.

6. There is no person hath been more bound to his sacred Ma^{ty} then himselfe, which both hee and his posterity after him, hee hopes, will ever with gratitude remember. All which is so notorious to the whole world, as that person must needes laugh at him, that should heare him say, his Ma^{ty} hath done nothing for him. And that he should speake of his Ma^{ts} person with contempt is the most foule untsults that can be uttered; for there are many noble persons, which I can produce, who in my private and most solemne communication with them have heard mee often and lately admire his Ma^{ts} great personall abilities, and particularly have heard mee say these very wordes, I protest, and before God,

I thincke and know the King himselfe to be a wiser man, and of greater judgment then any he advises withall. I can say no more but this, that my heart is and ever shall bee full of gratitude, for so many great obligations, which I owe to his sacred Matie; and that there is no man liuing that is more thoroughly perswaded of his great and personall partes then my selfe.

7. Hee never did goe about to vilify the actions of this Assembly, nor to perswade any not to giue obedience unto them, nor did euer lessen theyr power, unlesse it were in the sense formerly expressed concerning the full jurisdiction, as if they were the two entyre Houses of Parliament. Concerning which I may have sayd somthing, which I cannot remember.

That concerning the perswading men to teare out and embezill the Actes of that counsell, hee remembers that in jeast one morning in the House, in the presence of the Lord Keeper and many other Lords, hee did upon occasion say, that how could they aboue know who voted them traytors if the names in our clerkes booke were not to be seene? Upon which by approbacion of the laughter of all present, my Lord of Douer swore he would take order for it. This was a mere jeast openly done, and noe more concernes mee then any other present.

8. That many things which wee of late, especially in his Ma^ts absence, have had at the Counsell Table, were of such a publique nature, as concerning the mais^r, the workes, the towne and such other things as all men both know, before and after all the matter; and such things peraduenture I might speake of out of the Counsell, as everybody did. But that euer I did reveale any counsell of importance to any disaffected persons, I utterly deny.

9. To the last, I doe soe utterly deny every syllable in it, as I will loose my life if any one bee proved. I never so much affected to be of this treaty as ever to open my mouth to any man living, or use any meanes to bee. I hope it is in better and wiser hands, and I shall have the fruit of theyr laboures.

Indorsed: Copy of A Reply of the Earle of Sussex, written in his owne hand upon sight of the Reasons given by his Ma[ty] to the Lords for his confinement, shewen him this 28th of January, by his Ma[ts] command by mee,

EDW. WALKER.

PETITION OF VISCOUNT SAVILE.[a]

To the hon[ble] y[e] Com[ttee] for Compositions.
The petition of the Lord Viscount Savile.

SHEWETH,

Whereas y[e] pet[rs] estate hath bin long sequestred, and all his personall estate, goods, and houshold stuffe amounting to a great value seized and sold, and his house at Howley in y[e] County of York demolished, and his pson also imprisoned 26 weeks in Newark Castle by y[e] Earle of Newcastle, and afterwards sent to Oxford, and there imprisoned by his Ma[tie], and now since his voluntary coming in to y[e] parliament comitted to ye Tower, where hee hath bin a prisoner for many moneths, and of late hath bin and still is by reason of ye incurable disease of the stone in ye bladder in imminent danger of death.

Hee therfore praieth (being exceedingly desirous to leave his poore estate unincombred with this sequestraçon) you would bee pleased to admit him to composiçon, and to take into yo[r] iust consideration y[e] paps annexed, being most willing to submit to any thing the most Honble House of Comons and this Com[ttee] shall determyne concerning him.

And hee shall pray, &c.

SAVILE.

rec[d] M'ch 26, 1626 (*sic.* ? 1646).

---

a This petition and all the documents which follow are taken from the Royalist Composition Papers in the Public Record Office, Second Series, volume vi.

MICHAEL MIDDLEBROOKE.

I humblie certifie whome it may concerne that in October 1642, at Captain Hotham's comminge up from Caw-wood Castle into our partes of Yorkeshire, hee seized upon a trunke of my Lord Savile's, wherin (to my owne knowledge) there was three hundred and twentie poundes in monie besides divers suites of rich apparell, and other things of great vallew, which trunke he found at the house of Mr. Abraham Hinchcliffe, a tenant to my Lord Savile.

Within a few daies after I received order from my Lord to [pay] to the said Captaine Hotham fower hundred and twentie poundes more, which accordingly I pformed, takeing two men more with me, and carried the fower hundred and twentie poundes in money. and plaite and paid it to the said Capt. Hotham in Caw-wood Castle, according to an agreement betwixt himselfe and my Ladie Bland in my Lords behalfe. Upon the receipt of which somes Capt. Hotham did ingage himselfe to procure from y⁰ parliam⁰ a protection and freedome for his Lo^ps pson and estate.

All which I am able to prove, and shall be readie (God willing) to depose the same, if I shall be thereunto called.

Witnes my hand,
MICHAELL MIDDLEBROOKE.

Kerkstall Iron-workes,
this 4 of Aprill, 1646.

KATHERINE BLAND.

That in the be▮▮ of my Lord Savile I did treate withe Captayne Hotham and agreed withe him for the preservačon of his estate and protection of his person payeing him the some of a thousan poundes, wch was accordinglye payed and received by him. For Captayne Hotham himselfe att Leedes, in October 1642, confessed to me that he hadd received the some of 320*l.* in money besides apparell and other thinges of greate vallow, in a truncke of my Lord Saviles att the house of Mr. Abraham Hinchcliffe at Kerstall Abbey—the rest of the money wee agreed upon (Captayne Hotham being content to take that in the trunck in pte). I gave order to one Michaell Midlebrooke, a serv* of my Lords, to carrye to Cawood to Captayne Hotham, which he did accordinglye; for not onlye by word of mouthe but under his hand he did acknowledge the receipt of it, and did ingage himselfe to procure a protection from the parle*mt* or Close Cõmittee for his Lordshippes person and estate, which the said Captayne Hotham tould me he had power to doe. This agreem* betwixt Captayne Hotham and my selfe was in Sept*mbr*, 1642. All which I shall be readye to depose if I be theareunto lawfullye called.

Witnesse my hand this 8th of Aprill, 1646.

KA: BLANDE.

HENRY ANDERSON.

That being at Oxford, a prisoner, I hard the Lord Savile had beene accused for making a composition and paying certaine sommes of money to Captaine Hotham my sonne in law, whereuppon being afterwardes a prisoner in the tower w*th* Captaine Hotham I did demaund of him before his execution the truth of the said business, who then told me that he had made such an one w*th* the Ladie Bland in behalfe of the Lo. Savile, and had received therefore a certaine somme of money (what the particuler somme was he doth not now remember), and did allso declare unto him how he had disbursed some of the said moneyes to some particular officers of his armie.

Witnes my hand,

HEN: ANDERSON.

STATEMENT OF WILLIAM RISLEY.

May it please you, att the earnest importunity of Sir Peter
Temple, Knt., and his worthie and most virtuous Lady, I was over-
ruled to take an ill journey in a dirty season in the latter end of a
Michaelmas Tearme, about 3 years and odd moneths since, to
Yorke, to the Lord Savill, haveing noble Sr Phillip Stapleton's
letter to the younger Hotham to lett me passe (if pchance his forces
mett me), whither when I came I was, with the postboy of Tadcaster, carried before the Earle of Cumberland and others for our
examinacon. The postboy being first and apart strictly examined
(as I understood after) whether I had any conference with the Lord
Fairfax or any of his privately att Tadcaster (where then the said
Lord Fairfax kept garrison), which, when nothing by him appeare-
ing, I was for that night and p^{r}sent slenderly examined by them
concerninge my buisnes, and occasion of my tedious journey to my
Lord to Yorke ; and was dismissed with a small guard, but with
many watchfull ieyes over mee, to the posthouse, my lodging, without
any admission to my Lord Savill that night. And to my greate
amazem^t was rushed upon about one or two of the clocke att night,
my cloathes, bootes, and sadle, and my selfe searched to the skinn
for paps and instruccons ; but findeing nothing but a letter of the
Lady Temple to the Lord Savill concerninge law buisnes formerly
shewed them they left me for that p^{r}sent. I was, as soone as I
stirred in the morninge, carried againe before the Lord of Cumberland and others for further examinacon, which held long, soe that I
was not admitted to the speech of my Lord Savill till two or three
of the clocke in the after noone, whom after some passages and
enterchange of discourses betweene us found him most desireous to
come here to the parliamt (as I conceaved) with his severall
attempts to breake from them att Yorke, but was hindred and
p^{r}vented by their ielous ieyes over him in the towne, some
attending him aloofe of with horses after him, when as we went out
to take the aire. The Lord of Newcastle's horses alsoe being quartered

in places in about Yorke, the day after I came into Yorke (as we had intelligence in the towne), which sumerie of my now weake and obsoleete remembrance (by reason it is soe long agoe) I humbly then acquainted the right hono^{ble} the Lord Say with all att my returne and the very same to the best of my now remembrance att th'earnest request of my Lord Savill, I most humbly rep'sent now againe.

WILLIAM RISLEY.

THOMAS LORD VISCOUNT SAVILL MAKETH OATH.

That hee did not desert the parliament at that tyme when his Matie comanded all the members to attend him, which might shew like a designe to disolve the two houses, but long before when none but his Ma^{te} houshold servants did attend him, amongst which hee was a sworne servant and bound by oath to that attendance, and at y^t tyme when there was noe outward visible appearance of a warre on either side.

But hee saith that on the 6th of June, 1642, hee was voted a delinquent for a supposed misdemeanor committed in May before upon an informacon to the House of Comons out of Yorkshire, to which hee was never called to answere, neither was it true as it was prsented, as hee is able to prove by good testimony.

That at his being with his Matie at Yorke, when hee had pvided himselfe of armed guards, hee did, at the desire of some of ye Com^{ttee} of both Howses then resident at York, as an acceptable service to ye parliam^t as they alleadged pswade the King to dismisse them as looking to like a semblance of warre, wherein hee p'vailed wth his Matie, for which act hee was represented to ye parliam^t as two hon^{ble} psons then Com^{rs} from ye parliam^t did expresse unto him, and wch hee is confident they will upon occasion testifie. And when afterwards his Matie was at Beverley, intending to beseige.

Hull, hee did at ye desire of another com^{ttee} of both Houses use all his power to diswade his Matie from y^t resolučon though not with the like successe as before.

That when his Matie went to Nottingham to set up his standard this dep^t refused to goe wth him, but returned to his owne house, p^rsuminge for his good service aforesaid hee might have continued there in ye good opinion of the parliament.

But afterwards hee understanding from Capt. Hotham, then intrusted with ye parliam^{ts} forces, that hee was under the parliam^{ts} displeasure for ye misdemeanor aforesaid, unlesse hee would pay a some of money for a composičon hee must proceed against him as a delinquent, the said Capt. Hotham assuring him that hee had an absolute power to compound wth him and all other delinquents in those pts, even with my Lo. of Cumberland himselfe, wherupon hee treated with him, and at last concluded and agreed to give him 1,000*l.* to ye use of the State, the which he paid and satisfied accordingly, and therupon Capt. Hotham pmised to discharge him of his delinquency and pcure ye parliam^{ts} protection for him also.

That p^rsently afterwards the Earle of Newcastle came with his forces into Yorkshire and therupon Capt. Hotham retired into Hull, and by that means hee could not pforme his pmise in pcuring this deponent's discharge from ye parliam^t; and not long after the said Earle, having notice of the said composičon, caused him to bee app^rhended in the night with 200 horse, or thereabouts, under the comand of Sir Thomas Glemham and Colonel Causfeild, a Romish Catholique, and p^rsently carryed in ye night towards Newark, and there comitted a close prisoner.

That during the tyme of this dep^{ts} imprisonem^t the Earle of New Castle did goe in pson unto his house at Howley, in Yorkshire, and there upon a councell of warre, which hee then called, did seize and dispose of his goods as the goods of an enemye, and further did in a sort demolishe his house, to his damage above 10,000*l.*

That upon payment of his said composičon this dep^t did send up to ye Lady Temple to desire her to acquaynt some of ye parliam^t

wth his resolucon to come to London, wherupon one Mr. Risley was sent downe unto him to invite him to repaire thether, the wch hee attempted to doe, but could not effect by reason of ye great jealously ^{a} that was upon him.

That after 26 weeks imprisonem^t at Newark hee was sent a prisoner to Oxford together wth his accusacon, the two principall articles whereof were for his said composicon with Capt. Hotham and for voting against his^b comming into Yorkshire, all wch was shewed unto this dep^t from his Matie with intimacon that if his Matie should pceed vigorously against him it was not to bee answered.

That his Matie engaged him not to dept thence without lycence, in hope that at ye meeting of ye Assembly then shortly after being appoynted to come together, hee would deserve ye passing by of ye said offences and further merrit such other favors as his Matie had pmised and intended to conferre upon him.

That the said Assembly being met, in wch this dep^t not answering his Maties expectacon, nor deserving (as his Matie was pleased to say) his favor and lenity extended towards him, hee was againe comitted close prisoner at Oxford for about 3 moneths and impeached againe by his Matie himselfe for the composicon made with Capt. Hotham, and for contemptuously speaking against and villifying ye acts of that Assembly; and thereupon an impeachm^t of treason was p^{r}ferred against him by ye Lo. Digby in ye King's name, and a letter produced by his Matie under this dept^s owne hand to Capt. Hotham intimating his said composicon and his desire to have his discharge and proteccon of Parliam^t according to his pmise; upon w^{ch}, the judges being consulted withall and their opinion declared, it was moved in the open Assembly thatt hee might bee tryed by martiall lawe, but the Lords refusing to agree unto such a triall (hee being a peere of the realme), after some tract of tyme hee was released upon condicon hee should dept this kingdome.

That the very day after he was freed from imprisonm^t hee came towards London and voluntaryly (surrendered) himselfe unto y^e

---

^{a} *Sic.* ^{b} *i. e.* the Earl of Newcastle's. *See* p. 31, *post.*

parliam^t, wch was long before Naseby fight, when his Matie was in an outward probable way of successe.

That besides the composiĉon afores^d the parliam^t hath ever since ye battell neere York seized upon all his stock of iron, one pcell whereof (as hee is informed by his servants) was valued by the com^{ttee} at 1450l., besides his goods in London solde to their use also.

That his tenants, taking ye opportunity of his misfortune, destroyed his lands, wasted and made havock of his estate, and made it of small value, consisting more of stock then rent by reason of his iron works and tillage that hee managed.

That when ye Earle of Newcastle rifled his house the souldiers seized upon his writings and evidences, wherby hee is disabled to make ye certeynty of his title and estate appeare, but hath delivered in ye substance thereof to his best knowledge and remembrance.

SAVILE.

Jur. 27 die April, 1646.

JOHN PAGE.

LORD LOVELACE.

I John, Lord Lovelace, doth well remember that when I was with the Kinge at Oxford, and that the Lord Viscounte Savil was there, he knewe him to be in the Kinge's displeasure, and was for some times imprisoned, accused for treason, and the treason laid to his charge beinge for vilifyinge and speakinge slightly of that assembly at Oxford, and for compoundinge wth Captaine Hotham, and treatinge wth him about deliveringe upp of Yoarke, or to some such purpose; and for houldinge corespondence wth some heere at London; all wch I doe well remember and shall be reddy to verifie uppon occasion. As witnesse my hand this twenty-eight day of April, 1646.

JO: LOVELACE.

Thomas Lord Viscounte Savile maketh oath, that about the year 1634, hee being then violently prosequted in the Starchamber Court by some potent persons ill affected to him, did advice with his Councell Sir Henry Calthrop and Mr. Thorpe, a member of the Honourable House of Commons, to settle his estate in that manner whereby it might bee lesse subiect to those great fines wch did threaten him from them. And that his estate was thereupon setled in the hand of feffees in trust to himselfe for life the remaynder to his brother wch other remaynders over. And hee saith that hee was the rather induced thereunto by reason hee had no childe (neither yet hath any) nor possibility of any by his then wife, or probability of survyving her, shee being then in good health, and himselfe (as hee is now) much afflicted with the stone. And this dep^t further saith, that for more apparant evidence of the truth hereof, a treaty of marriage being with his now Lady (which was performed in the beginning of this parliam^t, and before theis warrs began), and hee being desired and desirous to make her a convenient joynture after his decease, did to that end submit his writings by which his estate was settled to the pusall of Mr. Beniamin Weston, Esqr (Father in law to this dep^ts now wife) and his councell, who upon his examinačon thereof told this dep^t that they found that hee had then no power to settle the joynture desired after his death. Whereupon hee gave assurance and satisfaccon by collaterall security, wch was accepted. And lastly this dep^t saith, that his writings concerning his estate were lost, when his house at Howley in Yorkshire was plundred by the Earle of Newcastle since the beginning of theis warrs, as is sufficiently knowne to Sr John Savile and many others who kept his said House for the parliam^ts use.

SAVILE.

Attestat sup honore et spontanee jurat, 4 Augusti, 1646.

ROBT. AYLETT.

STATEMENT OF THE DELINQUENCY OF THOMAS LORD VISCOUNT SAVILE.

That beinge his Ma^{ts} sworne servant, and long before there was any visible appearance of a warre, his absence from the parliam^{te} was occasioned by his personall attendance upon his Mat^{ye}, and when afterwards at Yorke his Matie provided himselfe of armed guards at a request of a com^{tee} of both howses then attendinge there, his Lo^{pe} did perswade the Kinge to have dismissed them, as havinge too like a semblance of warre, and afterwards again at Beverly did the like, and when his Ma^{tye} went to Nottingham to set up his standard he refused to goe along and retired to his owne howse, yet the 6^t of June, 1642, he was voted a delinquent by the Howse of Commons upon an informacõn from Yorkeshire of a misdemeanor supposed to have been comitted the May before, and doth nowe depose upon his oath that that informacõn was not true, as it was represented ; that afterwards he was notwithstandinge inforced by Captaine Hotham then in armes for the parliam^{te} to compound with him for that delinquency, who assured his Lo^{pe} that he had a full power from the parliament soe to doe, and not onely to compound with him, but with the Earle of Cumberland alsoe, and all others in those parts, to whom his Lo^{pe} paid 1,000l., and was thereupon promised by him to have a dischardge from the howses for that offence; and then his Lo^{pe} was resolved to come for London, and for that purpose sent hither and laboured his freinds heere to make way for his returne, who had such incouradgem^{te} therein that he made two severall attempts to have left the country and come upp, but was both tymes prevented. And shortly after the Earle of Newcastle tooke the field and enforced Captain Hotham to retire into Hull, and sent a party of 200 horse under the comaund of Sr Thomas Glemham and one Collonell Causfeild, a papist, who surprized him in his howse, and in the night tyme caryed him to Newarke, where he was comitted close prisoner, and lay 26 weeks

restraynd, his onely offence being his composicõn made with
Captaine Hotham, and for votinge against the Earle of Newcastle's
comeinge into Yorkshire. And after this tyme of imprisonmente
he was sent in custody to Oxford to the Kinge, and his l̃r̃es intercepted that passed betweene Captaine Hotham and him con-
cerneinge it, obiected against him by his Ma^tye at his comeinge
thither, and the same produced that after some reprehension his
Ma^tye gave him the liberty of the towne upon an ingadgem^te that
he should not depart thence without his licence ; and shortly after
that Assembly mett in which he noe waies answeringe his Ma^ts
expectation nor deserveinge (as his Ma^tye was pleased to say) his
highnes favors, he was againe comitted a close prisoner there at
Oxford ; and after a quarter of a year's tyme of imprisonm^te he
was impeached by his Ma^tye himselfe of high treason for makeinge
the said composicõn and for speakeinge against and vilifyinge the
Acts of the Assembly, and was indicted for the same, but upon a
consultation thereof had with the iudges they determined that the
said crimes obiected were rather tryable by martiall lawe, to which
the lords there would not agree; and then after some further tyme
lyinge in prison he was againe released upon his undertakeinge that
he should leave the kingdome, and then took an opportunity and
came to London, where he lyes now restraynd. All this matter
doe appeare by his Lo^pps affidavit, and by severall other certificates
and testimonialls subscribed under the hands of many noble par-
sonadges and others, testifyinge the same, and heereupon doth pray
that this matter may be specially reported togither with his fine,
hopeinge as his cause is to finde the favor of the howse therein.

He hath taken the nationall covenant and negative oath before
the Com^rs of the Greate Scale and before Samuell Gibson, minister
of Margaretts, Westm̃, the 28th of Aprill, 1646.

That he compounds upon a perticuler delivered in under his
hand, by which he doth submit to such fine, &c., and by which it
doth appeare :—

That his Lo^pe is seized of a franckten^te for life in possession, the

INDEX.

www.ingramcontent.com/pod-product-compliance
Lightning Source LLC
Chambersburg PA
CBHW021443090426
42739CB00009B/1616